B
B

God

can handle it

...Marriage

God
can handle it
...Marriage

Compiled and Edited by Dr. S. M. Henriques

BRIGHTON BOOKS
Nashville, TN 37205
1-800-256-8584

ISBN 1-887655-90-5

The quoted ideas expressed in this book (but not scripture verses) are not, in all cases, exact quotations, as some have been edited for clarity and brevity. In all cases, the author has attempted to maintain the speaker's original intent. In some cases, quoted material for this book was obtained from secondary sources, primarily print media. While every effort was made to ensure the accuracy of these sources, the accuracy cannot be guaranteed. For additions, deletions, corrections or clarifications in future editions of this text, please write BRIGHTON BOOKS.

Printed in the United States of America

Layout by Sue Gerdes & Criswell Freeman
1 2 3 4 5 6 7 8 9 10 • 97 98 99 00 01

For Mary Ann

Table of Contents

"The words of the wise are like goads, their collected sayings like firmly embedded nails— given by one Shepherd."
(Ecclesiastes 12:11, NIV)

Introduction

"Call on God, but row away from the rocks."

That's an old Indian proverb which reminds us that, while God has the ability to handle various circumstances in our lives, those of us who call on Him still have our own responsibilities.

St. Augustine phrased the same truth this way: "Without God, we cannot. Without us, God will not." Though Augustine was not speaking specifically of marriage, his words still apply. While God can handle anything we might face in our marriages, He will not do it alone.

This book contains relevant scripture verses and thought-provoking quotations about the sacred union between a husband and wife. These pages convey time-tested principles that work, but it's up to you (and your beloved) to make them work.

God can indeed handle your marriage, but the tools He chooses to use are such things as love, forgiveness, kindness, communication, and even adversity. As you explore this text and the ideas it contains, think of the various ways God invites you and your spouse to enter into a working partnership with Him to make your marriage all it can be.

1

The Essential Nature of Marriage

"Marriage is the only union that can't be organized. Both sides think they're management." This humorous viewpoint presents only one side. On the other hand, Mike Mason writes, "A marriage is not a joining of two worlds, but an abandoning of two worlds in order that one new one might be formed."

Learning to love and triumph in marriage is an ongoing process. If you're going to let God handle your marriage—if He is going to lead and guide you in this most wonderful of human relationships—then a proper and basic understanding of marriage and love is essential.

This chapter is not intended to be an exhaustive description of the nature of marriage. But perhaps it will make you hungry to find out more.

Marriage is...an exercise in amazement.

Mike Mason

*"This is it!" Adam exclaimed. "She is part of
my own bone and flesh! Her name is 'woman'
because she was taken out of a man.'"*
Genesis 2:23 (TLB)

Marriage is that relation between man and woman in which the independence is equal, the dependence mutual and the obligation reciprocal.

Unknown

Hail! Wedded love, perpetual fountain of domestic sweets!

John Milton

Marrying for love may be a bit risky, but it is so honest that God can't help but smile on it.

Josh Billings

Jesus said, "Not everyone is mature enough to live a married life. It requires a certain aptitude and grace."
Matthew 19:11 (The Message)

Marriage is the most natural state of man
and, therefore, the state in which you will find
solid happiness.

Benjamin Franklin

Plenty of people miss their share
of happiness, not because they never found it,
but because they didn't stop to enjoy it.

William Feather

Say "no" to the good so you can say "yes"
to the best.

Unknown

*Above all else, guard your heart,
for it is the wellspring of life.
Proverbs 4:23 (NIV)*

We tend to forget that happiness doesn't come as a result of getting something we don't have, but rather of recognizing and appreciating what we do have.

Frederick Koenig

Husbands, go all out in love for your wives.
Don't take advantage of them.
Colossians 3:19 (The Message)

Marriage is the greatest institution ever invented! It can be good, or it can be great, but it should never be ordinary.

Neil Clark Warren

A good woman is hard to find, and worth far more than diamonds. Her husband trusts her without reserve, and never has reason to regret it.
Proverbs 31:10-11 (The Message)

It is of the very essence of love that it be invisible and incomprehensible and a million light-years beyond us, and so much greater than we are that we swoon at its touch.

Mike Mason

Love makes everything lovely.

George Macdonald

After 6,000 years of human history, marriage always has been and still is the number-one relationship shared by the vast majority of people. No other relationship even comes close.

Tim LaHaye

Houses and wealth are inherited from parents,
but a prudent wife is from the LORD.
Proverbs 19:14 (NIV)

It is a marvelous thing when love comes bubbling up like tears in the throat as one is gripped by a sudden stabbing realization of the other's beauty and goodness, of how incredibly precious this person is.

Mike Mason

How beautiful you are, my darling!
Oh, how beautiful!
Song of Solomon 4:1a (NIV)

A beautiful woman appeals to the eye;
   a good woman appeals to the heart.
   One is a jewel; the other, a treasure.

Napoleon

A wife is a gift bestowed upon man
   to reconcile him to the loss of paradise.

Johann Wolfgang von Goethe

Among God's rich gifts to me are a twenty-four
hour day and dear family and friends. Surely
they were given to be spent on one another.

Susan Lenzkes

*A worthy wife is her husband's joy
and crown...
Proverbs 12:4a (TLB)*

There is no more lovely, friendly and charming
relationship, communion or company
than a good marriage.

Martin Luther

There is nothing in the world better than a
good marriage and nothing in the world worse
than a bad one.

Old-time Saying

Marriage is the salt of daily life.
It makes everything just a little bit better.

Dr. Joyce Brothers

*The LORD God said, "It is not good for the man
to be alone. I will make a helper
suitable for him."
Genesis 2:18 (NIV)*

Woman was not taken out of man's head to be lorded over by him, or from his feet to be trampled on by him, but from his side to be equal with him, from under his arm to be protected by him, and from near his heart to be loved by him.

Charles H. Spurgeon

So the LORD God caused the man to fall into a deep sleep; and while he was sleeping, he took one of the man's ribs and closed up the place with flesh.
Genesis 2:21 (NIV)

Marriage is the grafting together of two hearts, the planting of them in one another so that they become interdependent for their very lives. It is intended to be a picture of the way we all belong to Jesus, as branches to the vine.

Mike Mason

I am the vine; you are the branches.
John 15:5a (NIV)

The most successful marriages are those where both husband and wife seek to build the self-esteem of the other.

James Dobson

At the heart of personality is the need to feel a sense of being lovable without having to qualify for that acceptance.

Maurice Wagner

How far you go in life depends on your being tender with the young, compassionate with the aged, sympathetic with the striving, and tolerant of the weak and strong. Because some day in life you will have been all of these.

George Washington Carver

Out of respect for Christ, be courteously reverent to one another.
Ephesians 5:21 (The Message)

To be married is to be confronted intimately day after day with the mystery of life, of other life, of life outside of oneself.

Mike Mason

And the LORD God formed man from the dust of the ground and breathed into his nostrils the breath of life, and man became a living being.
Genesis 2:7 (NIV)

He who is filled with love is filled
with God Himself.

St. Augustine

Marriage is the perfection which love
aimed at, ignorant of what it sought.

Ralph Waldo Emerson

An ideal wife is any woman
who has an ideal husband.

Booth Tarkington

When a man finds a wife, he finds
something good.
Proverbs 18:22a (NCV)

Good marriages are made in heaven.

Old-time Saying

As a bridegroom rejoices over his bride, so will your God rejoice over you.
Isaiah 65:2 (NIV)

2

Spiritual Foundations

A do-it-yourself philosopher commented, "Marriage is a high sea for which no compass has yet been invented." But this statement is untrue for those who seek God's guidance. Thankfully, the One who "invented" marriage has also provided a compass for those who are willing to discover and use it.

Discovering the guidance of God in our marriages means that we may, from time to time, need to return to a few basic principles concerning our relationships with Him. The ideas which follow can serve as material for building a foundation that neither time, illness nor adversity can wash away.

A personal relationship with Jesus Christ is the cornerstone of marriage, giving meaning and purpose to every dimension of living.

James Dobson

But as for me and my household,
we will serve the Lord.
Joshua 14:15 (NIV)

A good marriage is not a contract
between two persons but a sacred covenant
between three.

Donald T. Kaufman

Marriage is a wonder! Nothing else in all of
creation pictures so adequately the relationship
between Christ and the believer. Nothing else,
in all of creation dramatizes so well the love,
intimacy and faithfulness God shares
with His people.

Rocky Henriques

Marriage ought to be a bond of love,
reflecting the love Christ has for His people, a
bond of sacrificial love where husband and wife
become one, one flesh, a unity.

Daniel Freeman

*Dear friends, let us love one another,
for love comes from God.
1 John 4:7a (NIV)*

We've grown to be one soul—two parts;
our lives are so intertwined that when some
passion stirs your heart, I feel the quake
in mine.

Gloria Gaither

God, the best maker of all marriages,
combines your hearts in one.

William Shakespeare

When spiritual bonding is established ...
the souls of two people
are woven together.

Neil Clark Warren

Has not the LORD made them one?
Malachi 2:15a (NIV)

Love is the fusion of two hearts — the union of two lives — the coming together of two tributaries.

Peter Marshall

Do two walk together unless they have agreed to do so?
Amos 3:3 (NIV)

You can put the past behind you once and for all by deciding that God has brought you together, and state to your spouse with firm conviction, "Yes, I believe God has brought us together, and I receive you as His gift to me."

Dennis and Barbara Rainey

I thank my God every time I remember you.
Philippians 1:3a (NIV)

Marriage is not a thing of nature
but a gift of God.

Martin Luther

The joining of a man and a woman in
matrimony is a supernatural event,
founded upon a mutual exchange
of holy pledges.

Mike Mason

Love has its source in God, for love is the very
essence of His being.

Kay Arthur

God is love.
1 John 4:16b (NIV)

Not from his head was woman took,
　　As made her husband to o'er look;
　　But fashioned for himself a bride;
　　An equal, taken from his side.

Susannah Wesley

People do not have to be alike to be equal.
The best way to destroy anything is to take
away its basic reason for being and making it
like something else. To seek to make woman
just like man is to destroy her reason for being.
God did not take Adam's rib and make another
man. He made a helper fitted to his needs.

Jack Taylor

Too many married people expect their
partner to give that which only God can give,
namely, an eternal ecstasy.

Fulton Sheen

*Therefore encourage one another and build
each other up, just as in fact you are doing.
1 Thessalonians 5:11 (NIV)*

If a couple were to seek the Lord …rejoice in Christian fellowship, and spend time both alone and together in prayer and study of the Scriptures, they would soon find their love-life filled with a rich glow and a mysterious new energy which cannot be discovered through any worldly means.

Mike Mason

Glorify the LORD with me; let us exalt his name together.
Psalm 34:3 (NIV)

Our homes are intended by God to reflect His glory; and when they do, then the love of Christ comes blazing through.

William Fitch

The LORD… blesses the home of the righteous.
Proverbs 3:33 (NIV)

The nearest thing to heaven on this earth is the Christian family and the home where husband and wife, and parents and children, live in love and peace together for the Lord and for each other.

M. R. DeHaan

The Good News is proclaimed by life as well as by lip, and since that is so, where can there be a better place for demonstrating the heart of the Good News than at the heart of a true marriage and a gracious Christian home?

William Fitch

When home is ruled by the Word of God, angels might be asked to stay with us, and they would not find themselves out of their element.

Charles H. Spurgeon

I have hidden your word in my heart that I might not sin against you.
Psalm 119:11 (NIV)

Marriage, as simply as it can be defined,
is the contemplation of the love of God in and
through the form of another human being.

Mike Mason

God has set the type of marriage everywhere
throughout the creation. Every creature seeks
its perfection in another. The very heavens
and earth picture it to us.

Martin Luther

God's creative act is constantly being
completed whenever marriage takes place
between a man and a woman.

William Fitch

*How great is the love the Father
has lavished on us...!
1 John 3:1a (NIV)*

Nothing is sweeter than love, nothing stronger, nothing higher, nothing wider, nothing more pleasant, nothing fuller or better in heaven or in earth; for love is born of God, and cannot rest but in God, above all created things.

Thomas á Kempis

My command is that you love each other
as I have loved you.
John 15:12 (NIV)

Love. No greater theme can be emphasized. No stronger message can be proclaimed. No finer song can be sung. No better truth can be imagined.

Charles Swindoll

And now these three remain: faith, hope and love. But the greatest of these is love.
1 Corinthians 13:13 (NIV)

Spiritual intimacy in marriage requires
both partners to submit to the leadership
and lordship of Christ, instead of competing
for control.

H. Norman Wright and Wes Roberts

Spiritual intercourse may be the highest
level of intimacy.

Gary Smalley

When two people cling to each other and
pour out their feelings to a God they both
trust and love, there is a merging and
blending that weaves them together
at their deepest levels.

Neil Clark Warren

But be sure to fear the LORD and serve him
faithfully with all your heart.
1 Samuel 12:14a (NIV)

God put greater tough-ness and aggressiveness in the man and more softness and nurturance in the woman — and suited them to one another's needs. And in their relationship He symbolized the mystical bond between the believer and Christ.

James Dobson

'For this reason a man will leave his father and mother and be united to his wife, and the two will become one flesh.' This is a profound mystery, but I am talking about Christ and the church.
Ephesians 5:31-32 (NIV)

3

Commitment in Marriage

Ben Franklin once observed, "Promises may get friends but 'tis performance that keeps them." This maxim is especially true when it comes to the promises a husband and wife make to each other as they begin their life together. They pledge to love, to understand and to be patient. Commitment sets the boundaries and establishes faithfulness.

The words found in this chapter are reminders of the absolute need for faithfulness in marriage.

Marriage is the down-to-earth dimension of romance, the translation of a romantic blueprint into costly reality.

Mike Mason

Now it is required that those who have been given a trust must prove faithful.
1 Corinthians 4:2 (NIV)

Nothing is more noble, nothing more venerable than fidelity. Faithfulness and truth are the most sacred excellences and endowments of the human mind.

Cicero

Character is the ability to carry out a good resolution long after the excitement of the moment has passed.

Cavett Robert

God's blueprint for marriage calls for an exclusive relationship between one man and one woman as they enter into a lifetime covenant.

Alistair Begg

Therefore, my dear brothers, stand firm.
Let nothing move you.
1 Corinthians 15:58a (NIV)

Love in its first and fullest vigor pledges itself to a total fidelity; and the continual observance of this leads on to an ever deepening and maturing love.

William Fitch

Nothing is easier than saying words. Nothing is harder than living them, day after day. What you promise today must be renewed and redecided tomorrow and each day that stretches out before you.

Arthur Gordon

Knit your hearts with an unslipping knot.

William Shakespeare

Let love and faithfulness never leave you; bind them around your neck, write them on the tablet of your heart.
Proverbs 3:3 (NIV)

Married love burns as fire, and seeks nothing more than the mate. It says, "I want only you."

Martin Luther

One chooses one's mate as one chooses one's God: forsaking all others, until death.

Mike Mason

Remain faithful to your partner for life. No exceptions!

James Dobson

Where you go I will go, and where you stay I will stay. Your people will be my people and your God my God.
Ruth 1:16b (NIV)

Marriage demands toughness, and toughness proceeds out of commitment. No marriage will ever be stronger than the commitment that serves as its foundation.

Neil Clark Warren

Husbands, love your wives, just as Christ loved the church and gave himself up for her.
Ephesians 5:25 (NIV)

Married life is a marathon, not a sprint. It is not enough to make a great start toward a long-term marriage. You will need the determination to keep plugging, even when every fiber in your body longs to give up. Only then will you make it to the end.

James Dobson

A faithful man will be richly blessed.
Proverbs 28:20 (NIV)

Things can be good anywhere, but they're
even better at home.

Jewish Proverb

There is no place more delightful
than one's own fireside.

Unknown

In order to say yes to absolute faithfulness,
we must say no to a number of other options.

Alistair Begg

*Marriage should be honored by all, and the
marriage bed kept pure…*
Hebrews 13:4a (NIV)

Love is a
great beautifier.

Louisa May Alcott

*Bless your fresh-flowing fountain! Enjoy the wife
you married as a young man! Lovely as an angel,
beautiful as a rose — don't ever quit taking delight
in her body. Never take her love for granted!
Proverbs 5:18-19 (The Message)*

Boys flirt. Mature men prefer more
meaningful and lasting relationships.
No one is incapable of being faithful,
but many are unwilling.

Abigail van Buren

Divorce merely substitutes a new set of
miseries for the ones left behind.

James Dobson

Rejecting divorce as an option allows for
great security in marriage. It means that when
problems arise — no matter how great those
problems may be — the couple will learn to
return to the instruction manual of God's
Word and rely upon the help of God's Spirit.

Alistair Begg

*Therefore what God has joined together,
let man not separate.
Mark 10:9 (NIV)*

Happy is the wife whose husband knows and tells her that if given the chance to marry all over again, he would choose the same bride.

Tim LaHaye

My lover spoke and said to me, "Arise, my darling, my beautiful one, and come with me."
Song of Solomon 2:10 (NIV)

The likelihood of survival is markedly improved when marriages are grounded in friendship, companionship, and the awareness of an unending covenant, no matter what.

Alistair Begg

Agree with each other. Love each other.
Be deep-spirited friends.
Philippians 2:2 (The Message)

4

Expressing Your Love

Learning to express love toward the most important person in your life does not always come easily. Sometimes, marital communication takes work ... and practice.

Robert A. Heinlein commented, "Love is that condition in which the happiness of another person is essential to your own." Helping *your* spouse discover his or her happiness will require the regular expression of *your* love.

It's no surprise that wise husbands and wives develop the habit of saying, "I love you" early and often. As Harvey Firestone said, "You get the best out of others when you give the best of yourself." His words apply to the expression of love. So make "I love you" a regular part of your marital communications. You'll be making two people happy.

God delights in changing lives and giving new beginnings. Your marriage can become a healthy, productive garden where two people generously express to one another gratitude, appreciation, belief and praise.

Dennis and Barbara Rainey

And this is my prayer: that your love may abound more and more in knowledge and depth of insight.
Philippians 1:9 (NIV)

Y‌ou will find as you look back upon your life that the moments that stand out, the moments when you have really lived, are the moments when you have done things in a spirit of love.

Henry Drummond

A‌ gentle touch or countless other tender expressions of "I care" separate love relationships from mere acquaintances.

Holly and Chris Thurman

L‌eaving my side of the road to come to yours is what caring is all about.

David Ferguson

Love...always protects, always trusts, always hopes, always perseveres.
1 Corinthians 13:6,7 (NIV)

There is no disguise which can hide love
for long where it exists, or simulate it
where it does not.

François de La Rochefoucauld

Love, the itch and a cough cannot be hid.

Thomas Fuller

Love and you shall be loved.

Ralph Waldo Emerson

Follow the way of love...
1 Corinthians 14:1a (NIV)

Love is the strange bewilderment which overtakes one person on account of another person.

James Thurber

His banner over me is love.
Song of Songs 2:4b (NIV)

Kissing is a means of getting two people
so close together that they can't see anything
wrong with each other.

G. Yasenak

The Kiss—Something made of nothing,
tasting very sweet.

M. E. Bueli

A kiss is a secret told to the mouth
instead of to the ear.

Edmond Rostand

Let him kiss me with the kisses of his mouth.
Song of Songs 1:2a (NIV)

The highest love of all finds its fulfillment not in what it keeps, but in what it gives.

Father Andrew

Mature individuals go into a marriage not only for what they can get out of it, but for what they can give to their partners.

Tim LaHaye

The wedding is merely the beginning of a lifelong process of handing over absolutely everything, and not simply everything that one owns but everything that one is.

Mike Mason

Consider the great love of the LORD.
Psalm 107:43 (NIV)

Love, like a lamp, needs to be fed out of the oil of another's heart, or its flame burns low.

Henry Ward Beecher

This is my lover, this my friend.
Song of Songs 5:16b (NIV)

Amazingly enough, many couples make
time for just about everything —
and everybody — but each other.

Zig Ziglar

When two people are deeply and vitally
in love, they become wildly important
to one another.

Neil Clark Warren

The best relationships are built up, like a
fine lacquer finish, with the accumulated
layers of many acts of kindnesses.

Alan Loy McGinnis

...for your love is more delightful than wine.
Song of Songs 1:2b (NIV)

Love is spontaneous and craves expression
through joy, through beauty, through truth,
even through tears.

Leo Buscaglia

There is no remedy for love but to love more.

Henry David Thoreau

Express your gratitude to each other
until it becomes habitual.

Neil Clark Warren

...for love is as strong as death.
Song of Songs 8:6b (NIV)

It is by loving, and not by being loved, that one can come nearest the soul of another.

George Macdonald

The true measure of loving...
is to love without measure.

St. Bernard of Clairvaux

A good marriage is one which allows for change and growth in the individuals and in the way they express their love.

Pearl Buck

Above all, love each other deeply.
1 Peter 4:8a (NIV)

It is absolutely necessary
for every human being to
be loved. Your partner
will never tire of hearing
you tell him or her
of your love.

Tim LaHaye

I ask that we love one another.
2 John 3b (NIV)

5

Being Married Takes Work

Former President of the United States Lyndon Johnson once quipped: "Only two things are necessary to keep one's wife happy. One is to let her think she is having her own way, and the other, to let her have it."

Actually, it takes quite a bit more than that. It's been observed that "All marriages are happy. It's the living together afterwards that causes all the trouble." That's what Helen Rowland meant when she wrote, "Marriage is like twirling a baton, turning handsprings, or eating with chopsticks. It looks easy until you try it."

Being married takes work, to be sure. And it is our work that God will use to strengthen and fortify the partnership we call marriage.

A great marriage requires carefully informed and precisely drilled participants who envision what they can have with one another and then set about the task of producing it in the relationship.

Neil Clark Warren

Make my joy complete by being like-minded, having the same love, being one in spirit and purpose.
Philippians 2:2 (NIV)

Marriage is an empty box.
It remains empty unless you put in more
than you take out.

Unknown

There are no shortcuts to any place
worth going.

Beverly Sills

If a marriage gives out, there usually hasn't
been enough put in.

Unknown

*Each of you should look not only to your own
interests, but also to the interests of others.
Philippians 2:4 (NIV)*

All that is needed to grow the most vigorous weeds is a small crack in your sidewalk. If you are going to beat the odds and maintain an intimate, long-term marriage, you must take the weeding task seriously.

James Dobson

Love does not die easily. It is a living thing.
It thrives in the face of all life's hazards,
save one — neglect.

John Dryden

Success consists of a series
of little daily efforts.

Mamie McCullough

And whatever you do, whether in word or deed,
do it all in the name of the Lord Jesus, giving
thanks to God the Father through him.
Colossians 3:17 (NIV)

Loving and living with your partner takes daily determination and practice — and the giving of oneself for the good of the other.

Tim LaHaye

Let us consider how we may spur one another on toward love and good deeds.
Hebrews 10:24 (NIV)

Being a Christian doesn't give you instant marital success. As Christ demonstrated, relationships take time and work.

Dave and Claudia Arp

...find out what pleases the Lord.
Ephesians 5:10 (NIV)

What you and your spouse need is plenty of plain old wonderful time. Quiet, uninterrupted, unhurried, stress-free time.

Neil Clark Warren

Just as a car does not continue to perform at maximum level if it is not serviced routinely, a relationship cannot maintain its maximum effectiveness if it is not given regular focused attention.

Clifford and Joyce Penner

Even marriages made in heaven need down-to-earth maintenance work.

Lloyd Byers

Let us not become weary in doing good, for at the proper time we will reap a harvest if we do not give up.
Galatians 6:9 (NIV)

Genuine love is a fragile flower. It must be maintained and protected if it is to survive.

James Dobson

Great marriages seldom come naturally. They are virtually always the result of strong motivation, careful instruction, and endless practice.

Neil Clark Warren

A marriage is old when two people feel that there is nothing more to discover together. Since there is always something new to share, most of the marriages that grow old are the ones that allow themselves to grow old.

David Viscott

Make every effort to keep the unity of the Spirit through the bond of peace.
Ephesians 4:3 (NIV)

I define a healthy marriage as two people who
have committed themselves to take individual
responsibility to work together
for the fulfillment of the other.

David Field

Talking to God about your husband
is an act of love.

Stormie Omartian

As grateful as a man may be for the guidance
and help he has received from his parents, it is
imperative for the well-being of all concerned
that he understands the importance of heading
up a whole new separate decision-making unit.

Alistair Begg

*For this reason a man will leave his father and
mother and be united to his wife, and they will
become one flesh.
Genesis 2:24 (NIV)*

Love convinces a couple that they are the greatest romance that has ever been, that no two people have ever loved as they do, and that they will sacrifice absolutely anything in order to be together. And then marriage asks them to prove it.

Mike Mason

How beautiful you are and how pleasing,
O love, with your delights!
Song of Solomon 7:6 (NIV)

6

The Need to Communicate

Communication is multi-colored. It comes in all shapes, forms and sizes. It is delivered through lengthy conversations, muttered words, the posture of one's body, or even silence. H. Norman Wright knew this when he wrote, "Communication is both talking and silence; it is touching and a quiet look."

But it's even more than that. It's also sharing, and caressing, and praying, and gazing. It can be done in tender, gentle ways, or in a rough, uncaring manner.

Whether we know it or not, the lines of communication are always open. In this chapter we'll learn how to keep those lines *straight*.

Couples who are successful as lovers are successful not by accident but because they have learned how to communicate.

Dennis Guernsey

*Be gracious in your speech. The goal is to
bring out the best in others in a conversation,
not put them down, not cut them out.
Colossians 4:6 (The Message)*

The most crucial issue in a marriage
is not that a couple communicate,
but what they communicate.

Walter Wangerin, Jr.

Good communication comes when you
value and take the time to understand
your differences.

Jerry D. Hardin and Dianne C. Sloan

If there is any indispensable insight with
which a young married couple should begin
their life together, it is that they should try
to keep open, at all cost, the lines
of communication between themselves.

Reuel Howe

*Patient persistence pierces through indifference;
gentle speech breaks down rigid defenses.
Proverbs 25:15 (The Message)*

Silences make the real conversations
between friends. Not the saying but the never
needing to say is what counts.

Margaret Lee Runbeck

Married couples who love each other tell
each other a thousand things without talking.

Chinese Proverb

The true test of being comfortable with
someone else is the ability to share silence.

Frank Tyger

...a time to be silent and a time to speak...
Ecclesiastes 3:7 (NIV)

Words are like seeds.
Once planted in your
mate's life, your words
will bring forth flowers or
weeds, health or disease,
healing or poison.

Dennis and Barbara Rainey

The tongue has the power of life and death...
Proverbs 18:21a (NIV)

Communication in marriage isn't that
complicated. It's not difficult;
it's just hard work.

Dennis Guernsey

As terrific as pillowtalk is, it has to be
backed up by kitchen talks and sofa talk, the
"I'm home, honey" talk, daily-walking-together
talk, or comfortable nontalk — seas of peace
and quiet, sharing holy space.

Lib Uzzell Griffin

Good communication takes time.

Les and Leslie Parrott

*Kind words are like honey — enjoyable and
healthful.
Proverbs 16:24 (TLB)*

To keep your marriage brimming,
 With love in the loving cup,
 When you're wrong, admit it,
 When you're right, shut up.

Ogden Nash

Seek to be a plow rather than a bulldozer. The plow cultivates the soil, making it a good place for seed to grow. The bulldozer scrapes the earth and pushes every obstacle out of the way.

John Maxwell

Communication is to love what blood is to life.

H. Norman Wright and Wes Roberts

Pleasant words are a honeycomb, sweet to the soul and healing to the bones.
Proverbs 16:24 (NIV)

P sychologists say it is impossible
to distinguish intense listening from love.

Bruce Larson

I believe that virtually every marriage in
North America would be several times better
if the two people were simply to improve
their listening skills.

Neil Clark Warren

*Let your conversation be gracious as well as
sensible, for then you will have
the right answer for everyone.
Colossians 4:6 (TLB)*

7

Being Best Friends

My wife is my best friend!

The kind of love that lasts is a love that enables a wife and her husband to be best friends with each other. They may not always agree and may sometimes become angry with each other. But their friendship remains.

Of course, husbands and wives will have other friends. But if everyone else turns away, the partners in marriage will still have each other. And know it. And depend upon it.

Great marriages are graced by an almost mystical bond of friendship, unbreakable commitment, and a deep understanding that nearly defies explanation.

James Dobson

Just as lotions and fragrance give sensual delight, a sweet friendship refreshes the soul.
Proverbs 27:9 (The Message)

One of the main motivating factors toward marriage is the need to feel complete because of what the other person has to offer.

H. Norman Wright and Wes Roberts

The best friend is likely to acquire the best wife, because a good marriage is based on the talent for friendship.

Friedrich Nietzsche

Love is friendship set on fire.

Jeremy Taylor

Two are better than one, because they have a good return for their work.
Ecclesiastes 4:9 (NIV)

The goal in marriage is not to think alike
but to think together.

R. C. Dodds

All that I love loses half its pleasure
if you are not there to share it.

Clara Ortega

Passionate love is a fragile flower;
it wilts in time. Companionate love is a sturdy
evergreen; it thrives with contact.

Elaine Walster and G. William Walster

*Friends come and friends go, but a true friend
sticks by you like family.
Proverbs 18:24 (The Message)*

When two people form a partnership that is bathed by caring and love, and when they are sufficiently healthy within themselves so that they don't put pressure on the marriage to perform functions for which it is incapable, a fantastic marriage is just around the corner.

Neil Clark Warren

Though one may be overpowered, two can defend themselves. A cord of three strands is not quickly broken.
Ecclesiastes 4:12 (NIV)

A friend is one to whom
one may pour out all the
contents of one's heart,
knowing that the gentlest
of hands will take and sift
it, keep what is worth
keeping, and with a
breath of kindness, blow
the rest away.

Unknown

*Greater love has no one than this, that he lay
down his life for his friends.*
John 15:13 (NIV)

8

Learning to Deal with Conflict

An old African proverb tells us that "when the elephants fight, it's the grass that suffers." When a husband and wife encounter conflict, their relationship can be trampled underfoot. But not necessarily.

Conflict comes in many packages and occurs for a variety of reaons. But the fact remains that conflict does exist in a marriage. Can God handle it? Of course He can! But God will "handle" marital conflict only in partnership with the husband and wife. The verses and the quotations in this chapter show how God handles our conflicts ... by handling us.

Yes, Virginia, there are times in every good marriage when a husband and wife don't like each other very much.

James Dobson

Let us therefore make every effort to do what leads to peace and to mutual edification.
Romans 14:19 (NIV)

Conflict is a necessary part of every marriage
for as long as that marriage lasts.

Neil Clark Warren

Conflict is inevitable. What matters is
how it is handled.

Michael J. McManus

No disagreement is a threat to a marriage; it's
what a couple does about disagreements that
determines the success or failure of a marriage.

Tim LaHaye

A dry crust eaten in peace is better than steak
every day along with argument and strife.
Proverbs 17:1 (TLB)

Marriage has taken a bum rap because a lot of untrained, undisciplined, uninspired, and sometimes unhealthy people have tried it and failed.

Neil Clark Warren

There is no mistake so great as that of being always right.

Samuel Butler

A quarrel is quickly settled when deserted by one party; there is no battle unless there be two.

Seneca

Don't have anything to do with foolish and stupid arguments, because you know they produce quarrels.
2 Timothy 2:23 (NIV)

We don't marry into an instant understanding of each other.

Dave and Claudia Arp

Blessed are the peacemakers, for they will be called sons of God.
Matthew 5:9 (NIV)

When love is strong, a man and woman can
make their bed on a sword's blade;
when love is weak, a bed of sixty cubits
is not wide enough.

The Talmud

In a sense, a marriage lives and dies by what
you might loosely call its arguments, by how
well disagreements and grievances are aired.
The key is how you argue — whether your
style escalates tension or leads to
a feeling of resolution.

John Gottman

Keep working on the conflict until you both
feel good about the solution.

Gary Smalley

*You do well to be angry — but don't use your
anger as fuel for revenge. And don't stay angry.
Don't go to bed angry. Don't give the Devil that
kind of foothold in your life.
Ephesians 4:26-27 (The Message)*

When you give your relationship priority over the two individuals that make it up, conflicts become a challenge that, when handled successfully, will enhance and strengthen your union.

Neil Clark Warren

Do nothing out of selfish ambition or vain conceit, but in humility consider others better than yourselves.
Philippians 2:3 (NIV)

Many women could learn from men to accept some conflict and difference without seeing it as a threat to intimacy, and many men could learn from women to accept interdependence without seeing it as a threat to their freedom.

Deborah Tannen

Your attitude should be the same as that of Christ Jesus.
Philippians 2:5 (NIV)

9

Extending Forgiveness

Conflict between a husband and wife makes forgiveness necessary. Neither one is always right; neither one is always wrong. Victor Hugo wrote, "The supreme happiness of life is the conviction of being loved for yourself, or more correctly, being loved in spite of yourself."

God is never more involved in a marriage than He is when forgiveness is offered freely and regularly by both wife and husband. Forgiveness is what He uses to bring us closer to Him; it's also what He uses to bring us closer to each other. Indeed, there can be no lasting human relationship, in marriage or otherwise, where forgiveness is absent.

One unknown sage said, "Happiness lies in the backyard, but it's probably well hidden by crabgrass." God calls upon us to extend the hand of forgiveness. And when we do, we never allow the crabgrass of an unforgiving spirit to obscure the happiness that exists in our own backyard.

A woman who can't forgive should never have more than a nodding acquaintance with a man.

Ed Howe

If he sins against you seven times in a day, and seven times comes back to you and says, "I repent," forgive him.
Luke 17:4 (NIV)

Forgiveness is not a feeling but a choice
we make, and often it goes against every
self-centered fiber of our being.

Linda Dillow

You will need courage to forgive and lots
of practice, but forgiveness is something
you can learn.

Patrick and Connie Lawrence

Forgiveness is giving love when there is no
reason to love and no guarantee that love
will be returned.

Walter Wangerin, Jr.

Do not say, "I'll pay you back for this wrong!"
Wait for the LORD, and he will deliver you.
Proverbs 20:22 (NIV)

He who forgives first, wins.

William Penn

Love is an act of endless forgiveness,
   a tender look which becomes a habit.

Peter Ustinov

Learn how to apologize and how to forgive.

Neil Clark Warren

*Bear with each other and forgive whatever
grievances you may have against one another.
Forgive as the Lord forgave you.
Colossians 3:13 (NIV)*

He who forgives ends the quarrel.

African Proverb

It requires only an ounce of grace and a thimble full of brains to hold a grudge; but to entirely forget an injury is truly beautiful.

Unknown

"I can forgive, but I cannot forget" is only another way of saying, I will not forgive. Forgiveness ought to be like a cancelled note: torn in two and burned up, so that it never can be shown against one.

Henry Ward Beecher

A man's wisdom gives him patience; it is to his glory to overlook an offense.
Proverbs 19:11 (NIV)

Marriage is three parts love and seven parts forgiveness of sins.

Langdon Mitchell

*Be kind and compassionate to one another,
forgiving each other, just as in Christ
God forgave you.
Ephesians 4:32 (NIV)*

10

Practicing Patience and Kindness

There's an old story of the man who came home from work, kissed his wife warmly, and offered to help with preparing supper. The wife burst into tears, exclaiming, "What a rotten day this has been! Little Tommy broke his arm, the washing machine broke down, and now you come home drunk!"

Hmmmm. If you treated your spouse with warmth and kindness, demonstrating patience when it's needed most — would he or she have reason to be suspicious?

Two qualities — patience and kindness — are back-to-back characteristics of the Fruit of the Holy Spirit as described in Galatians 5: 22. They should be a normal part of any marriage. The quotations and verses on the next few pages will remind us all of the need for patience and kindness. And lots of it!

Keep thy eyes wide open before marriage, and half-shut afterwards.

Benjamin Franklin

*Be completely humble and gentle; be patient,
bearing with one another in love.
Ephesians 4:2 (NIV)*

W e have committed the Golden Rule
to memory; let us now commit it to life.

Unknown

B e kind to one another: This is the Golden
Rule of marriage and the secret of making
love last through the years.

Randolph Ray

T he secret of a happy marriage is simple:
Just keep on being as polite to one another
as you are to your best friends.

Robert Quillen

Here is a simple, rule-of-thumb guide for behavior:
Ask yourself what you want people to do for you,
then grab the initiative and do it for them.
Matthew 7:12 (The Message)

Shall we make a new rule of life: always try
to be a little kinder than necessary.

Sir James Barrie

Kindness is a language which the deaf
can hear and the blind can see.

Mark Twain

There are no traffic jams in the second mile.

Unknown

*If someone forces you to go one mile,
go with him two miles.
Matthew 5:41 (NIV)*

The Creator who began with nothingness and made beautiful mountains and cuddly little babies has elected to give us the inside story on the family. Marriage and parenting were His ideas, and He tells us in His Word how to live together in peace and harmony.

James Dobson

Therefore, as God's chosen people, holy and dearly loved, clothe yourselves with compassion, kindness, humility, gentleness and patience.
Colossians 3:12 (NIV)

The difference between a successful marriage and a mediocre one sometimes consists of leaving about four or five things a day unsaid.

Unknown

I have never known a happy henpecked husband, nor have I ever met a happy henpecker.

Tim LaHaye

You can have a dinner table with every delectable delicacy and the bounty of each season, but if the emotional tone around the table hangs heavy with unpleasantness, you might as well be eating leftover pizza from somebody else's party.

Les and Leslie Parrott

Better to live alone in a tumbledown shack than to share a mansion with a nagging spouse.
Proverbs 21:9 (The Message)

Minor irritants, when accumulated over time, may even be more threatening to a marriage than the catastrophic events that crash into our lives.

James Dobson

Don't let the seeds spoil your enjoyment of a watermelon. Just spit out the seeds.

Unknown

No life can be complete that fails in its little things. A look, a word, a tone of voice even, however small they may seem to human judgment, are often of vital importance in the eyes of God.

Hannah Whitall Smith

Above all, love each other deeply, because love covers over a multitude of sins.
1 Peter 4:8 (NIV)

To forbear replying to an unjust reproach, and overlook it with a generous, or if possible, with an entire neglect of it, is one of the most heroic acts of a great mind.

Joseph Addison

Love is patient, love is kind.
1 Corinthians 13:4a (NIV)

11

When Adversity Comes

Many years ago, William Shakespeare penned, "Love is an ever-fixed mark that looks on tempests and is never shaken." We agree. Love is the one thing that enables us to keep pushing forward when everything else is crumbling around us.

If the love of a husband and wife is true, the appearance of adversity actually strengthens their love. Gary Smalley has written, "Suffering has a way of bringing people together; the most important things on earth come into sharper focus."

Since none of us are exempt from trouble, let us prepare ourselves in advance, knowing that adversity can make a marriage stronger.

Remaining tender during a trial is one of the most powerful ways to build an intimate relationship.

Gary and Norma Smalley

May the Lord make your love increase and overflow for each other....
1 Thessalonians 3:12a (NIV)

A marriage lives, paradoxically, upon those almost impossible times when it is perfectly clear to the two partners that nothing else but pure sacrificial love can hold them together.

Mike Mason

Perhaps true love can best be recognized by the fact that it thrives under circumstances which would blast anything else into small pieces.

E. Havemann

Trust is what enables couples to flourish in the good times and hold together through the bad times.

Neil Clark Warren

Love never fails.
1 Corinthians 13: 8 (NIV)

Weather the storms of life by turning toward
one another and building into each other
rather than rejecting one another.

Dennis and Barbara Rainey

No man knows what the wife of his bosom
is until he has gone with her through
the fiery trials of this world.

Washington Irving

A loving marriage is a solid guarantee that
no matter what else may happen, at least
there will be some love in the world.

Mike Mason

*I look up to the hills, but where does my help
come from? My help comes from the LORD,
who made heaven and earth.
Psalm 121:1 (NCV)*

The formula for achieving a successful relationship is simple: You should treat all disasters as if they were trivialities, but never treat a triviality as if it were a disaster.

Quentin Crisp

Do not worry about anything, but pray and ask God for everything you need, always giving thanks.
Philippians 4:6 (NCV)

Renew your commitment — especially when the going gets hard.

Neil Clark Warren

Let us hold firmly to the hope that we have confessed, because we can trust God to do what he promised.
Hebrews 10:23 (NCV)

The darkest hour is only 60 minutes long.

Unknown

When everything seems gray,
          look for the color.

Cherry Hartman

The night is not forever.

Unknown

*Even if I walk through a very dark valley, I will
not be afraid, because you are with me.
Psalm 23:4a (NCV)*

Though weary, love is
not tired; though pressed,
it is not straitened;
though alarmed,
it is not confounded.
Love securely passes
through all.

Thomas á Kempis

*We have troubles all around us, but we are not
defeated. We do not know what to do, but we
do not give up the hope of living. We are perse-
cuted, but God does not leave us. We are hurt
sometimes, but we are not destroyed.*
2 Corinthians 4:8-9 (NCV)

12

Sex: The Amazing Gift

God knew exactly what He was doing when He made us different! Our sexuality is a part of God's original intention, as demonstrated in the very design of our bodies. It was not added on as an afterthought.

In this chapter we consider one of God's amazing gifts: the sexual relationship between a wife and a husband.

God gave the gift of sex like a precious jewel to humanity — the crown of all His creation.

William Fitch

I belong to my lover, and his desire is for me.
Song of Solomon 7:10 (NIV)

The Bible teaches that sex is a creation of God and an excellent thing to be enjoyed within the bounds God has set for it.

Sherwood Wirt

Sex provides a means of presenting one's spouse with the gift of oneself and experiencing a like gift in return.

H. Norman Wright and Wes Roberts

Happy is the woman who looks upon the act of marriage as a means of showing her love for her husband and of his showing his love for her. In a vital sense it may be the only single experience she and her husband have together in which they do not have to share each other with another person.

Tim LaHaye

The husband should fulfill his marital duty to his wife, and likewise the wife to her husband.
1 Corinthians 7:3 (NIV)

If you're going to have a romantic affair,
have it with your mate!

Dave and Claudia Arp

Sex should never be something a man does
to his wife but an experience they share
together, providing them the greatest single
pleasure that they can enjoy throughout their
entire lifetime. It is a gift of God,
meant for our good.

Tim LaHaye

Sex inescapably is one of the holiest shrines
of life, a crossroads of towering spiritual
intensity where simple but monumental
decisions are made and acted out, choices
that have earth-shattering ramifications for
every detail of a life.

Mike Mason

*You have stolen my heart with one glance
of your eyes...
Song of Solomon 4:9b (NIV)*

The whole idea was God's.

William W. Orr

*Sex is as much spiritual mystery
as physical fact.
1 Corinthians 6:16 (The Message)*

The deep spiritual significance of sex speaks
of the fellowship between Christ
and his church. There is deep expression,
communication, and satisfaction
in this fellowship.

Jack Taylor

In the plan of God, sex was intended to
provide a means of totally revealing oneself
to the beloved, of pouring one's energies
and deepest affection, hopes, and dreams
into the loved one.

H. Norman Wright and Wes Roberts

*What is clearest to me is the way Christ treats
the church. And this provides a good picture of
how each husband is to treat his wife, loving
himself in loving her, and how each wife is to
honor her husband.*
Ephesians 5:32-33 (The Message)

In all fully Christian marriages, there should be the full enjoyment of sex as God gave it and as He meant it to be enjoyed. To deny it is to deny a gift that has capacities for untold good.

William Fitch

Do not deprive each other except by mutual consent and for a time, so that you may devote yourselves to prayer. Then come together again so that Satan will not tempt you because of your lack of self-control.
1 Corinthians 7:5 (NIV)

The woman who would never think of serving her husband the same microwave dinner every night sometimes serves him the same sexual response time after time after time. Sex, like supper, loses much of its flavor when it becomes totally predictable.

Linda Dillow

It takes time to communicate, to work through conflict, and to build a creative love life.

Dave and Claudia Arp

If you make your lover feel loved, you will significantly strengthen your marriage.

Neil Clark Warren

A bundle of myrrh is my well-beloved unto me; he shall lie all night betwixt my breasts. Song of Solomon 1:13 (KJV)

"Male and female He created them" (Genesis 1:27). So special a thing was this in God's eyes that he saved it until last, until all the rest of His creative work was in place.

Mike Mason

So God created man in his own image, in the image of God created he him; male and female created he them.
Genesis 1:17 (KJV)

As the desert traveller finds refreshment at the oasis where the well is deep and the water cool, so may man and wife be refreshed by one another.

William Fitch

Drink water from your own cistern, running water from your own well... May your fountain be blessed, and may you rejoice in the wife of your youth.
Proverbs 5:15, 18-19 (NIV)

13

Enduring Love

Nothing is more encouraging to the rest of us than to see a couple still in love after many years of marriage. This kind of enduring love serves as an example for any young couple seeking to carve out a life together.

Helen Hayes once commented that love "is perhaps the only glimpse we are permitted of eternity." Mark Twain hinted at this when he wrote, "No man or woman knows what perfect love is, until they have been married a quarter of a century." Love, if it is real, endures. It stands tall and straight through the years.

Been married a long time? George Elliot said, "It is never too late to be what you might have been." And it's never too late to make a marriage what it might have been. Here's how.

Love isn't like a reservoir. You'll never drain it dry. It's much more like a natural spring. The longer and the farther it flows, the stronger and the deeper and the clearer it becomes.

Eddie Cantor

Many waters cannot quench love;
rivers cannot wash it away.
Song of Solomon 8:7a (NIV)

I have developed a lifelong love for my wife,
but it was not something I fell into.
I grew into it, and that process took time.

James Dobson

They that love beyond the world
cannot be separated by it. Death cannot kill
what never dies.

William Penn

Marriage is a lifelong process
of discovering each other more deeply.

Ingrid Trobisch

*So Jacob served seven years to get Rachel,
but they seemed like only a few days to him
because of his love for her.
Genesis 29:20 (NIV)*

Getting married is easy. Staying married is more difficult. Staying happily married for a lifetime should rank among the fine arts.

Roberta Flack

Someone has written that love makes people believe in immortality, because there seems not to be room enough in life for so great a tenderness, and it is inconceivable that the most masterful of our emotions should have no more than the spare moments of a few years.

Robert Louis Stevenson

Don't miss love. It's an incredible gift.

Leo Buscaglia

*The LORD has done great things for us,
and we are filled with joy.
Psalm 126:3 (NIV)*

Chains do not hold a marriage together.
It is threads, hundreds of tiny threads,
which sew people together through the years.
That is what makes a marriage last —
more than passion or even sex!

Simone Signoret

Where you start is not as important
as where you finish.

Zig Ziglar

The love we have in our youth is superficial
compared to the love that an old man has
for his old wife.

Will Durant

We love because he first loved us.
1 John 4:19 (NIV)

We should measure
affection, not like
youngsters by the ardor
of our passion, but by its
strength and constancy.

Cicero

*And over all these virtues put on love, which
binds them all together in perfect unity.
Colossians 3:14 (NIV)*

Every enduring marriage involves an unconditional commitment to an imperfect person — your spouse.

Gary and Norma Smalley

As it turns out, abstinence before marriage and life-long fidelity were pretty good ideas after all.

James Dobson

Love should be a tree whose roots are deep in the earth, but whose branches extend into heaven.

Bertrand Russell

Let no debt remain outstanding, except the continuing debt to love one another...
Romans 13:8a (NIV)

Such a large and sweet fruit is a complete
marriage that it needs a long summer to ripen
it, and then a long winter to mellow
and season it.

Theodore Parker

To keep a fire burning brightly there's one
easy rule: keep the two logs together, near
enough to keep each other warm, and far
enough apart — about a finger's breadth —
for breathing room. Good fire,
good marriage — same rule.

Marnie Reed Crowell

I shall love you in December with the love
I gave you in May!

John Alexander Joyce

*My command is this: Love each other
as I have loved you.
John 15:12 (NIV)*

It takes years to marry
completely two hearts,
even of the most loving.
A happy wedlock is
a long falling in love.

Theodore Parker

Love one another deeply, from the heart.
1 Peter 1:22b (NIV)

A successful marriage requires falling in love many times, always with the same person.

Mignon McLaughlin

*May your unfailing love rest upon us, O LORD,
even as we put our hope in you.
Psalm 33:22 (NIV)*

Index of Quotations
by Source

Quotations by Source

About the Author

Dr. S. M. Henriques, known to his friends as "Rocky," lives and writes in Jackson, Mississippi. He is a graduate of New Orleans Baptist Theological Seminary with 20 years experience as a pastor.

Dr. Henriques is the author of *God Can Handle It ... Marriage* and *God Can Handle It For Kids,* both published by Brighton Books. He is also publisher of *The Timothy Report,* an internet newsletter for pastors.

Dr. Henriques is married with two children.

About Brighton Books

Brighton Books is a publisher of inspirational, Christian-based books. The company is located in Nashville, Tennessee. Brighton Books are distributed by Walnut Grove Press.

About the "God Can Handle It" Series

This book is part of a series called *God Can Handle It*. Each book in this collection combines inspirational quotations with relevant scripture passages. For more information about these or other titles from Brighton Books, please call 800-256-8584.